# Calm
## IN THE
# FACE
## OF
# CONFLICT

## Cheryl A. Cage

## Cage Consulting, Inc.
Business & Career Consulting • Publishing

**Other Titles by Cheryl A. Cage/Cage Consulting**

- Your Job Search Partner: A 10 Day, Step-by-Step, Opportunity Producing, Job Search Guide
- Checklist for Success: A Pilot's Guide to the Successful Airline Interview
- Checklist CD: An Interview Simulator
- Reporting Clear?: A Pilot's Interview Guide to Background Checks & Presentation of Personal History
- Mental Math for Pilots (McElroy)
- Airline Pilot Technical Interviews (McElroy)
- Pilot Classroom Series—AIM, FAR (McElroy)

---

Practical Strategies for Professional and Personal Growth

Calm in the Face of Conflict
Twelve Powerful Strategies to Help You Think Through Problems, Decisions, and Conflicts
By Cheryl A. Cage

© 2002 by Cheryl A. Cage

ISBN: 0-9714266-1-9

Library of Congress Control Number: 2002091260

**Disclaimer**
The author and publisher are not medical or legal professionals. This book does not offer, recommend, or provide any medical, mental health, or legal advice. The strategies it contains are applicable for the everyday conflicts, decisions, and issues that the majority of people face on a regular basis. It is understood that the information contained in this book does not guarantee success. The author and publisher shall have neither liability nor responsibility to any person or entity with respect to any loss or damaged caused, or alleged to be caused directly or indirectly by the information contained in this book.

The author and publisher are not presenting these twelve strategies as a panacea. They will *not* eliminate all your problems or give you mystic insight into every decision you face. Nor can they eradicate the inevitable conflicts everyone experiences as a member of the human race.

If you need medical, mental health, or legal advice, please consult a licensed, qualified professional. Problems such as physical or emotional abuse, drug or alcohol addiction, marital difficulties, and serious family or relationships problems may well require the assistance of a licensed counselor or psychologist. If you are faced with any of these situations, seek professional help immediately.

If you not wish to be bound by any of the above statements, you may return this book to the publisher for a full refund of the purchase price. Please contact the publisher at 1-888-899-2243 for book return information.

# Contents

# Development of the Twelve Strategies

As a young adult, I suffered from a bad case of "foot in mouth" disease. I immediately shared every thought or idea that popped into my brain with anyone in earshot. I rarely edited my comments and, looking back on my behavior, in some perverse way I suppose I viewed myself as uncommonly honest.

The turning point came when I was hired as a flight attendant right out of college. I found myself constantly surrounded by coworkers I didn't know, and in an environment where we had to work well together as a team. It soon became obvious that my "think-thought, share-thought" approach was not working well, as I found myself constantly having to explain my initial comments, "What I meant was. . . ." I never meant to be rude or impatient, but that's exactly the picture my unedited comments were painting.

I then found myself moving in the opposite direction. I rarely spoke up for fear that I would say the wrong thing. Being one to enjoy a good conversation this approach wasn't working well either. It was then that I made the conscious decision to pay more attention to what I *wanted* to say to people before I actually *said* it. To my delight, I found myself becoming a better communicator plus I was faced with fewer misunderstandings and conflicts. I was able to speak my mind, but I shared my comments with more maturity and compassion.

Fast forward to fifteen years later, when I was asked to present a seminar on problem-solving at one of my favorite conferences, Women in Aviation. (I must admit I chuckled a little when first approached.) Although how to work through difficult issues was a frequent topic of discussion in my individual consultations with my pilot-clients, this was the first time I had been asked to present a formal workshop on the subject to a group of professionals, most of whom were *not* pilots.

In the audience would be owners of aviation-related businesses (everything from aviation bookstores to aircraft parts warehouses), human resources professionals, vice-presidents of airlines and aircraft manufacturers, airline dispatchers, mechanics, schedulers, flight attendants, women just starting their careers, and seasoned professionals. All were professional women in the still largely male-dominated field of aviation—not exactly the type of people who have difficulty making up or speaking their minds! To be truthful, I was a little nervous that I would have anything new to share with this audience.

As I searched for an entertaining way to discuss handling problems, decisions, and conflicts, I began thinking about my early struggle to become a better communicator. I realized that, although I begun the process of editing my comments on my own, over the years I had *greatly enhanced* my communication and interpersonal skills by using the same practical strategies many of my pilot-clients employed.

Because pilots carry heavy responsibilities on their shoulders, one of the requirements for success is an ability to recognize potential mistakes, problems, and conflicts early, and then, to reach a resolution in a timely manner. In reviewing my own style, I came up with twelve specific problem-solving strategies I had learned from, or had enhanced through, consulting with pilots. I decided to share these twelve surprisingly straightforward, practical strategies with my audience.

My concern about audience interest was unwarranted. The strategies struck a common chord. Over the next several months, I received numerous requests for copies of the speech. People asked me to consult with them about specific problems they were facing, or important decisions they had to make. Many asked, "When are you going to write a book on these strategies?"

Let me share with you some experiences related by audience members:

---

**A young professional who was frustrated with having a pet project repeatedly rejected by her manager wrote:**

*I took your advice and spent some time critiquing why my project continued to be rejected. I then asked for a formal meeting with my manager. I feel that by using your techniques I will get the project accepted. I'll keep you posted.*

Three weeks later, in my morning e-mail, I read:

*The meeting was a success! I believe my manager was just waiting to see what type of plan and follow-through I would present. I am trying to be humble about this—thanks again for the advice.*

---

**A mid-level professional who was disenchanted with her job wrote:**

*Some of the points you made in your talk appeared to be directed at me. In applying several of the strategies, I realized I'm frustrated because I'm bored. I also realized I was spending a lot of time complaining and little time thinking creatively about what type of outcome I was really searching for. I'm not exactly sure what solution I will decide on, but it feels good knowing there is a solution out there.*

---

**A young professional who needed to discuss a sensitive problem with a supervisor wrote:**

*Thanks again for the great advice you offered regarding how to approach my supervisor.*

*I waited until the end of the day and asked him if we could speak in private. I was nervous, but I had thoroughly planned what I wanted to say. I told him of my concerns and the comments I had overheard from other employees. To my surprise he was very receptive. He said he hadn't realized his behavior was a problem.*

*I offered him some research I had gathered to help him with his problem and asked him to keep me informed. All in all, it was a very positive experience for both of us, and I'm glad I had the courage to speak up.*

---

These individuals had fretted for weeks about their particular problems. The twelve strategies proved to be the tools they needed to "jump start" their decision-making process and discover a solution that was best for them.

Over the course of the next year, I began to track when at least one of the strategies proved to be an important starting point toward solving (or alleviating) a troublesome issue. I discovered that one or more of the twelve strategies were applicable in 95% of the situations I and my clients faced. I kept notes on what worked particularly well and jotted down poignant or interesting stories that would help make a point clearer to a future client.

I am convinced of the universal utility of these twelve common-sense, straightforward strategies. If you make the effort to incorporate these strategies into your normal pattern of thinking, you will be amazed how much more confidently you will solve problems, resolve conflicts, and reach decisions. And, let's face it, solving problems in a quicker, cleaner manner will just naturally help to make your days calmer.

# Reader Outlook, Author Promise

As you read this book, I ask you to read with an open mind. Through the many stories I offer look for personal behaviors that seem familiar to you. An objective recognition of your behavior is the first step in implementing positive change.

My promise to you is twofold:

1.  To share real-life scenarios that may help you recognize your own problem-solving and decision-making weaknesses *and strengths.*

2.  To offer you proven, common-sense strategies that can help you to think through your decisions, problems, and conflicts in a composed and focused manner.

You will notice that some strategy descriptions are longer than others. The length of a chapter *does not* correspond to the relative importance of the strategy. All twelve strategies are important; some simply need a bit more discussion than others to ensure clarity. Also, the number assigned to the strategy does not suggest that these strategies must be implemented in any particular order.

I would never suggest that these twelve strategies are a panacea. They cannot eliminate all your problems or give you prophetic insight into every decision you face. Nor will they eradicate the inevitable conflicts and issues that arise in human relationships.

What these twelve strategies *can* do is to help you gain perspective by learning to recognize when you are overreacting and when your response is justified. They can also help you become a more systematic and effective decision maker and empower you to implement your chosen course of action in a calmer and more confident manner.

---

Problems such as physical or emotional abuse, drug or alcohol addiction, marital difficulties, and family problems may well require the assistance of a licensed counselor or psychologist. If you are faced with any of these situations, please do not hesitate to seek professional help immediately.

_____

# Build a Solid Foundation

---

**Build:** *to develop, promote, or strengthen*

---

As you become familiar with the twelve strategies in this book, I believe you will agree they are surprisingly straight-forward. You may discover, however, that they take some finesse to implement effectively when your blood is either boiling or running cold! For these strategies to become second nature, you must first build an appropriate foundation upon which they can flourish. This foundation is also made up of a surprisingly simple suggestion: **learn to slow down.**

To become proficient at responding purposefully rather than emotionally when confronted with a difficult situation, you must first become comfortable with taking your time in non-emotional situations. For the next week, your goal is to realize that *you control* your emotions (and thus your reactions); your emotions do not control you.

I challenge you to take one week to focus strictly on slowing down. If you take my challenge seriously, by the end of the week, I am confident you will discover that taking a few extra moments to complete any task rarely makes much difference in the long run.

Here are a few suggestions for how you can make taking your time second nature.

- Rise thirty minutes earlier in the morning. Spend these moments alone having your first cup of coffee, taking a walk, or simply reading the paper. *Begin* your day on a calm note.

- When driving, stay in the slower, right-hand lane; don't try to beat yellow lights. Allow another driver to move in front of you when you find lanes merging.
- Make a habit of acknowledging the people with whom you come into contact. Make eye contact, say "good morning," and make a little small talk. Notice what is going on around you.
- During conversations, listen to everything the speaker is saying *before* you begin to formulate your response. Allow others to complete their thoughts before you answer. Make a mental note when you interrupt others and strive to go one whole day without interrupting anyone!
- When running errands, park your car a little farther away from your destination. Take an extra minute or two to enjoy the walk to the entrance.
- Turn your cell phone off whenever possible.
- Don't watch TV or work before you go to bed. Give yourself at least twenty minutes of quiet time before turning out the lights.

If you can get into a rhythm of slowing down when things are going well, when faced with a difficult situation, it will be much easier to find the few extra moments you need to control your emotions. When you are comfortable moving at a relaxed pace, the remaining eleven strategies will become much easier to implement.

*One of the chores I hate the most is organizing the company checkbook. I arrived at the office early one morning to tackle two month's worth of checkbook business. As I began, I realized that my assistant had used the check numbers out of order. I was furious, because it made my job so much harder. Luckily for me, because it was so early, she had not yet arrived at the office. I kept working on the checkbook and about twenty minutes later realized I was the one who had used the checks out of order! I thanked my lucky stars that I hadn't been able to call my assistant into the office to point out 'her' mistake.*

Easy to see why it is so important to move slowly when faced with a situation that raises your blood pressure.

# Use Silence Effectively

---
***Effect:*** *the power to produce results*
---

After a week, hopefully, you are taking your daily life a bit more slowly. Now you want to begin to use this slower pace to your advantage.

Reacting immediately to any problem or conflict is rarely to your benefit (except in an emergency). For this reason, the following Time Principles should almost always be your first course of action when faced with a conflict, problem, or decision.

When someone does or says something that raises your blood pressure, your immediate reaction is likely to be 95% emotion and 5% fact. To become an effective and strategic problem solver, you must reverse these percentages. Let me suggest two Time Principles to help you reach a 95% *fact,* 5% *emotion* response.

## Time Principle 1:
## Silence, Please

Have you ever gotten *into* trouble by keeping your thoughts to yourself for a few extra minutes? No? So, when you are faced with a situation that makes you angry, hurt, or confused keep quiet for at least three minutes. During this time, visualize an image of "letting off steam" in your mind. For example, see your head as a teapot, with steam coming out of your ears, releasing the pressure of the moment.

Once you have successfully kept quiet for three minutes, decide whether you really need to say or do *anything* at that moment. If you decide something *must* be said or done, you will find your comments will be delivered in a much calmer and more reasonable manner.

> *When I first started my career, I shared an apartment with a colleague I'd met in training. We didn't know each other very well and seldom saw each other. I came home unexpectedly one day to find my roommate and her boyfriend relaxing on the patio. As I sat down to chat, I noticed my roommate wearing a jade ring that looked exactly like the one my mother had given me.*

> *My initial reaction was to reach over and yank the ring off her finger but, quite frankly, I was in shock and couldn't seem to move. I sat for several minutes in disbelief. To my surprise, my anger began to subside and my common sense took over. After a few minutes I said to her, "Is it possible that you are wearing my mother's ring?" Needless to say, she was horrified that she'd been caught and apologized profusely.*

> *I accepted her apology, but during those few minutes of thought, I had resolved to find another place to live. I had also realized that if I ranted and raved, our relationship would be unbearably tense until I could move out. During the few weeks it took me to find another apartment, my roommate was very polite to me. We were civil and there was no discussion of why I was moving. We both knew why. Because I had been able to control my anger, I was able to make the transition much more comfortably than I could have if I had exploded—as I had wanted to at first!*

## Time Principle 2:
## 23 Hours and 57 Minutes More Silence, Please

If you decide the situation is *not* time sensitive, I invite you to take your silence one step further. Keep your thoughts and feelings to yourself for twenty-four hours—"sleep on it."

> *A client confided that his wife, Charlene, reacted emotionally to every event. Her tendency to overreact had become so upsetting to him that he began to withhold sharing problems with her. He simply couldn't handle the ranting that accompanied every problem*

*(no matter how small). He admitted, however, that in the long run, she usually came up with the perfect solution to the problem.*

> **No one ever got *into* trouble by keeping their opinions to themselves for a few extra minutes.**

*Their life became much calmer as Charlene learned to listen carefully but keep her initial reactions to herself for twenty-four hours. Time Principle 2 helped her keep her initial, damaging overreactions in check, while allowing the marriage to benefit from her solid decision-making abilities.*

Use this twenty-four hours of quiet time to search for perspective (Strategy 3). After this review it is common to realize one of three things:

1. **The course of action that seemed perfect twenty-four hours ago doesn't seem so perfect now that your thought process is not clouded by emotion.** You realize that implementing your initial plan would not have been the best course of action. (Take a moment to congratulate yourself and to breathe a sigh of relief that you didn't start down that path.)

2. **Your initial course of action is appropriate, but the hiatus has given you time to compose your response.** You are able express yourself more coherently and effectively because you took the time to calm down and rehearse your response.

*Many years ago, I had a valued employee who did not show up for work and never called. I was out of town that day and was very disturbed that no one answered the phone at the office. Consequently, I spent an inordinate amount of my day trying to locate this employee (being concerned that something bad had happened), listening to voice messages, and returning phone calls.*

*I cut my trip short and arrived at the office at around 7 p.m. I had more than forty phone calls to return. At about 8 p.m., the employee walked through the door. At that point I was so angry and had so much work to do, I just said, "Help me return these phone calls."*

*The next day when the work was done and things were back to normal, I was able to have a calm, straightforward conversation with her. I said what needed to be said, but my comments were much more organized and delivered with reason and not emotion.*

3. **You realize that the best course of action is to do nothing.** Saying nothing is, at times, a valid solution.

*As a junior flight attendant I had to work every major holiday (New Year's Eve through Christmas). One Christmas holiday I was paired with a flight attendant whom I had never met. When I introduced myself, she was extremely unfriendly. "Oh," I thought, "she's probably upset about working Christmas."*

*It soon became obvious, however, that she was much colder toward me than the rest of the crew. I decided that I would try to break the ice by helping her with her work when I had completed my duties. When I did so, she found fault in everything I did even going so far as to make a sarcastic remark to me in front of a passenger. It was not the time or place to confront her, so I simply removed myself from her area of the aircraft.*

> **Just imagine how much calmer *everyone's* lives would be if we all waited twenty-four hours before voicing our opinions.**

*As I thought about her behavior that evening I realized that, having just met her, I couldn't possibly have said or done anything to offend her. I finally came to the conclusion that I probably resembled someone she despised! Yes, her treatment of me was rude and unprofessional, but she did not conduct herself similarly with others. As she was based in a different city we, most likely, would never work together again. I decided that the best solution was to leave the situation alone. Trying to talk to her probably would only make things worse by putting her on the defensive. For the rest of the trip I was cordial but kept our conversations to a minimum. We got along fine.*

## Careful of the 'Send' Button

E-mail has made our lives easier in many ways. On the other hand, it also creates one more avenue for us to embarrass ourselves or hurt other people's feelings, especially because written words are much easier to misinterpret without the voice or body language cues present in phone or face-to-face communication. *Always* wait twenty-four hours when you receive an e-mail that makes your blood pressure rise. Also, hit that "Send" button with caution. The

**Always wait twenty-four hours before hitting the "Send" button.**

sarcastic e-mail about your boss could really do some damage if you accidentally hit the "Send to All" button!

Need another reason to incorporate the Time Principles into your day? You will spend less time wishing you could take back words said during an emotional outburst.

# Seek Perspective

---
***Perspective:*** *evaluation of different points of view*

---

A bonus of implementing the Time Principles *first* is you then have plenty of opportunity to search for perspective. When confronted with an unpleasant situation (especially if you have been embarrassed or inconvenienced) it is easy to fall into the trap of reviewing the situation from one perspective only: *how the problem affects you.* I call this your *inward view.*

"There two sides to every story" may be a cliché, but it is absolutely true. The inward view is simply your side of the story. Your inward view is important because it helps you answer vital questions such as: Have I been treated unfairly? Are my feelings about this situation justified?

When trouble begins to brew and misunderstandings escalate is when the inward view is the *only* view you consider in searching for a solution. An objective and systematic problem solver must also take the time to view an issue with an *outward view:* viewing the problem through the other person's eyes.

Using the outward view, you can ask yourself an important question: How has *my* behavior contributed to the problem? You will usually find you are *not* the only person affected by the situation. To gain true and proper perspective on any problem or conflict, you must always consider both the inward and outward views.

*One of Ann's major responsibilities as member services coordina-tor for Vista Golf and Country Club was to purchase clothing for the member shop. She had ordered a casual golf shirt that came in several bright colors. When the shirts arrived, she decided to wear one in order to gauge customer response, even though the employee dress code called for more formal attire. The shirts sold out within two hours.*

*She decided to wear the shirt again the following week. That morning the club was crowded with members and employees when her boss walked in. Seeing her in the golf shirt he said, "I didn't say anything when you wore that shirt once, but you know it's not company-approved attire. Don't wear it again." All conversation ceased.*

*Ann was humiliated.*

At this moment Ann was at a fork in the road of problem solving. She had three distinct choices: (1) react to her feelings of humiliation by following her boss into his office and giving him a piece of her mind; (2) follow Time Principle 1 *but* use the time to fume about how poorly her boss treated her; or (3) use Time Principles 1 and 2 as opportunities to reach some perspective on what just happened by taking both an inward and an outward view. She chose the latter.

**Inward view: your side of the story**

Ann's inward view ("Is my reaction justified?") gave her confidence that, yes, she was justified in being irritated with her boss. In the more than five years she had worked for him, she had never been anything but a dependable, mature, and honest employee. She deserved more respectful treatment.

However, after taking an outward view ("How did I contribute to this problem?") Ann realized her boss also had a valid reason to be irritated with her.

Even though her intentions were good, she had known the shirt was not company-approved attire. And, after five years, she definitely knew how strongly her boss felt about appropriate business dress. She also had to admit that she had seen two other employees wearing casual shirts much like the one she wore. Using the outward view she was able to objectively recognize that her behavior had started a trend that put her boss in an awkward position.

Having calmed down and thought about the situation from both sides, Anne phoned her boss and asked for an appointment to speak with him the next day. When they were alone she said:

*"First, I would like to apologize for wearing non-approved attire to work. My reasoning was simply to promote the shirt to our members. We have sold out both days I wore it. However, I realize I should have come to you first and asked your permission. If I had done that, we probably wouldn't be having this conversation and I apologize for that.*

*At the same time, I respectfully request that when you have something negative to say to me or need to talk to me about my performance, you speak to me in private. I was extremely embarrassed in front of all those people."*

There! Ann apologized while at the same time making it clear how she expected to be treated. Her boss not only accepted her apology but also apologized for having embarrassed her.

## Practicing the Outward View

> **Outward view: the other person's side of the story**

The inward view is easy, but the outward view—now that can take some practice. To become proficient in pursuing the outward view use the Time Principles to mentally step back from the emotion of the moment. During this time, reverse the camera view to focus on yourself. Make a concerted effort to see the problem from the other person's point of view. Here's an opportunity for practice:

*A month ago, you offered to host a company dinner at your home. Unfortunately, two days before the party, your spouse comes down with a nasty flu. First thing in the morning, you inform the administrative assistant that you will be unable to host the party. His immediate response is a loud and irritated, "Well, that's just great. Nothing like waiting until the last minute!"*

- What's your inward view?

- Now try to think like the Administrative Assistant. What is his view of the moment (outward view)?

Here are some possibilities:

> **(Your) Inward view:** "Jeeze. I didn't do this on purpose. My husband is really sick. It's only a party."

> **(His) Outward view:** "Just great! Now I have to find a restaurant or arrange for a room and catering, and contact twenty people about the change of plans. Then I'll have to call the bakery and have the cake delivered to the new address. How am I going to do all this and put together the sales figures for the end of month?"

Having looked at both views how could you have presented the bad news in order to minimize the conflict?

> **Possible Approach:** By recognizing *in advance* the difficulties your announcement will make, you could pair the bad news with an offer of help: "Andrew, I'm really sorry, I know this is short notice, but my husband is completely down and out with the flu. I'm afraid our house isn't going to be available for the dinner. Now, what can I do to help you make new arrangements? Can I take responsibility for finding somewhere else to hold the party?"

With an acknowledgement of Andrew's dilemma and an offer to take responsibility for some of the difficulty the last-minute change would cause, you probably could have avoided the whole unpleasant incident.

Your problem-solving process will never be complete without a clear, realistic picture of both sides of the story. Recognizing other people's points of view empowers you to respond in a fair, realistic, and mature manner. The more you practice "tuning in" to other people's outlooks, the more easily you will be able to uncover a realistic solution.

# Recognize Unrealistic Expectations

---

*Recognize: to accept as a fact, admit*

---

Nothing stands in the way of moving forward with your life, relationships and goals more than unrealistic expectations. Unrealistic expectations waste precious time, energy and add frustration to your daily life.

> *More than anything Tom wants to work for the local TV station. He has a newly minted degree in communications, and an uncle that handles advertising for the station. He has asked his uncle to introduce him to the station's Human Resources Director, but his uncle has yet to arrange the meeting.*

Tom's unrealistic expectation of believing that his uncle is going to lay the groundwork for him is causing frustration on several levels. He's angry with his uncle for not being more 'supportive', and he's frustrated because his job search is stagnant because he has not gained an introduction to the HR Director. He is living with the unrealistic expectation that other people have as much time to invest, and interest in, his career goals as he does!

Because of his unrealistic expectation Tom is exhibiting behavior that is counterproductive to reaching his goals. He is wasting time being angry with his uncle instead of taking control of his own destiny by looking for additional ways to introduce himself to a decision-maker at the station.

> *Shari has spent the last seven years as a stay-at-home-mom. Now that her children are in school full-time she is anxious to get back*

*into retail store management. However, Shari has not kept her computer skills up-to-date. After several job interviews Shari is absolutely sure that the reason she is not being offered jobs is because employers have a grudge against women who have stayed home with their children.*

Instead of taking a few weeks and enrolling in some computer classes, Shari wastes her time exhibiting counterproductive behavior by moaning about how no one is giving her a chance. Until she recognizes that her expectation of being given 'on the job training' is unrealistic the likelihood of landing a management position is slim.

Let's do some in-depth review of several scenarios that illustrate common unrealistic expectations and counterproductive behavior. (Notice the use of both Inward and Outward Views.)

---

**Unrealistic expectation:** wanting a guarantee of success

**Counterproductive behavior:** spending too much time researching a problem to avoid taking action

---

I worked with a young woman who said her dream was to become an airline pilot. Over the course of several months, we had numerous brainstorming sessions to determine a way she could leave her current job in order to pursue flight training full-time.

After several lengthy brainstorming sessions she told me she was ready to put our plan into action. A few days later, however, she called with a dilemma: "Well," she began, "I thought I had this all worked out. But I just discovered that when I take a leave from my job, I will have to pay $200 a month for my health insurance."

While not discounting the fact that $200 is a lot of money, I suspected that this was simply one more excuse for this young woman not to make a final decision. She was extremely bright and perfectly capable of finding a part-time job that would allow her to earn the necessary money. As we talked, I learned she did indeed have other options that would provide not only enough to live on but also fairly good health benefits. I had been right; the insurance payment was only an excuse. I gently pointed out her propensity to want all the stars and planets to be perfectly aligned before she was willing to make a decision.

This young woman spoke unwaveringly about her desire to be a professional aviator—so why was she constantly setting up roadblocks? I suggested that she take a long, hard look at her reasons for wanting to become an airline pilot. Did she really love flying, or did she just like the idea of saying she was a pilot? Was she willing to do all the hard work required to reach her goal, or, in reality, did she lack the motivation and energy to pursue such a big challenge?

When I asked her these questions, her enthusiasm for flying never faltered. However, she began to talk at length about her fear that if she didn't succeed as a pilot, she would have given up a good job, placed herself in debt, and left herself without a career. It became clear that she was waiting for some guarantee of success before making a commitment.

We objectively reviewed her qualifications for problems or weaknesses that would make failure likely (barring the unexpected catastrophe). She was young and healthy, had gained four pilot licenses in ten months without failing any of the necessary written or flight tests (so, she was smart), and had a college degree. Hmm, no, there wasn't any logical reason to anticipate failure.

I then posed this question: "Picture yourself as a very, very old woman sitting on your front porch sipping a cup of tea. Which would cause you *no* regrets: (1) having spent your life working at a good non-flying job because you decided not to pursue becoming a pilot, or (2) having tried your hardest to become a pilot but having failed?"

Her answer was immediate: "Oh, I have to try! I'll take failure any day over not trying." Once she understood that no one could ever give her a guarantee that she would reach her goals, but that not trying was not an option for her, she was able to move forward with her plans. She realized that although there were no guarantees, her plans were based on realistic, solid facts.

Within two weeks she took a leave of absence and signed up for classes in meteorology to enhance her flight planning skills. She recontacted a well-known flight school that had previously been hesitant to give her a flight instructing job but, with a renewed sense of purpose, she talked her way into employment. I know she is going to succeed.

---

**Unrealistic expectation:** not wanting to experience disappointment

**Counterproductive behavior:** denying the depth of your desire to reach your goals

---

*A young pilot had been turned down by several airlines. By the time I met him, he was so fearful that he would never be offered a position that he had begun to deny his ambition. He projected the attitude, "If they don't hire me, I guess it was just not meant to be. It will be their loss."*

No. It was definitely going to be his loss.

I pointed out to him that his indifferent attitude was inconsistent with the fact that he had flown across the country to meet with me and try to figure out what was going wrong.

We finally realized he was so fearful of disappointment that he had begun to deny the strength of his aspirations in order to protect himself. If he talked himself into *not* wanting this career, the disappointment wouldn't hurt so much if he was rejected. By hiding behind a lackadaisical attitude, however, he was coming across as if he could care less about being an airline pilot. Talk about a self-fulfilling prophecy.

After several hours of discussion, we identified some elementary errors he had made during his first interviews, errors that could easily be rectified. We also discovered that after the initial rejections, he had added to his problems by projecting an attitude of aloofness. He quickly acknowledged that enthusiasm was a requirement for selection, a requirement he was not exhibiting. In order to be competitive, he needed to be willing to reveal, to himself and to others, that he wanted to be an airline pilot with every fiber of his being. If he didn't allow himself to fully experience how much he wanted this job, no interviewer would ever see his desire. The catch-22 is when you "give it your all," yes, it will hurt if you meet with failure—but failure is almost certain if you don't give it your all.

This young man corrected his initial interviewing errors. He arrived at his next interview with high hopes and high enthusiasm—and was hired by the airline.

---

**Unrealistic expectation:** To expect to reach a goal without making the necessary effort

**Counterproductive behavior:** denying one's weaknesses

---

In this next example let's take a more in-depth look at a person who decides to alleviate her UE and CB (as listed above).

*Barb recently found herself single again after many years. As she adjusted to her new role, she spent some time taking stock of her life. Because she and her partner had enjoyed a full social life over the years, she was surprised to discover that, on her own, she had not cultivated many friends.*

### Barb's Inward View

I am a very nice person. I am extremely generous and always available to do a favor. I have always gone out of my way to be friendly; people should like me!

### Outward View of Barb

Barb has overcome the first hurdle in solving her problem: she honestly wants to discover why she is lacking in friends. She must now search for the outward view.

She could start by reviewing her memories of recent social events: With whom did she talk? What did they talk about? Did she enjoy the conversation? Does she have any idea whether the other person enjoyed the conversation?

If she is unable to find any answers on her own, she then must turn to someone who knows her well and whom she trusts. Yes, this might be an uncomfortable exercise, but Barb has to be willing to take these risks, if necessary, to find out why she hasn't formed any lasting friendships.

### Outward View Discovery

In reviewing recent social situations, Barb realized that she had no idea whether the other person was enjoying the conversation, although she had definitely enjoyed it. As she analyzed other people's reactions, she began to notice that most of her memories were of people listening to her. Hmm, could this be a problem?

In fact, Barb had hit the nail on the head. Had she asked her acquaintances, they would have unanimously said, "She talks too much." "She's a nice person but I cringe when I see her number on the caller I.D.! I know if I answer I'm in for a two-hour conversation."

### Changing Counterproductive Behavior

Having uncovered her propensity to dominate conversations, Barb was able to identify a behavior she wanted to change. She decided to have a luncheon, inviting several people she had known for a long time. Without mentioning her soul-searching to anyone, she decided to strive not to talk for more than thirty seconds at a time. In addition, she prepared a list of questions that she could ask to encourage others to talk about themselves.

### Barb's Outcome

The luncheon was a success. The conversation flowed freely, with everyone contributing. It was difficult for Barb to keep quiet for that long a period, but she saw that people were opening up to her. Plus, she learned things about her acquaintances she had never known. She felt very good about the way she had handled the luncheon.

## EXERCISES

To discover if you are harboring some unrealistic expectations and counterproductive behavior, spend some time thinking through the following questions. As you review these questions strive to uncover personal expectations and behaviors that could be causing you to become embroiled in more unfulfilling and difficult situations than are necessary. If you can be honest with yourself, you will be well on your way to alleviating many of the problems and conflicts that plague your days.

Read through these questions once and quickly jot down your first reactions. Don't spend a great deal of time on them until you have read this entire book at least once. Remember, the purpose of this exercise is not to make you feel bad about yourself; we all have weaknesses (even me)! However we cannot instigate change until we acknowledge that change is needed.

## Ask Yourself

1. How do I voice my opinions, concerns, or displeasure?
   - Are there subjects that immediately raise my blood pressure?
   - Do people take any approaches with me that always "raise the hackles on my neck"?
   - Do I have trouble getting others to understand my point of view?
   - Do I have difficulty speaking honestly to people about my feelings?
   - Do I keep a lot of my comments and feelings bottled up because I don't want to "make waves"?
   - Do I regularly avoid people I am upset with?

2. How do I approach others?
   - If I remember people's birthdays, do I expect them to remember mine?
   - Does it irritate me when people don't take things as seriously as I do?
   - Do I celebrate differences in other people? Do I allow my friends, spouse, and children to be themselves? Or do I constantly feel the need to change their behavior and opinions?
   - Am I a giving conversationalist? Do I allow others to talk, or do I tend to dominate a conversation?

3. How do I handle making decisions?
   - Do I find it difficult to reach a conclusion?
   - Do I procrastinate when trying to make a decision?
   - Once I make a decision, how long does it take me to implement it?

4. Are there common themes to my mistakes or conflicts?
   - Am I constantly fighting the same battles or making the same mistakes?
   - Are there certain people with whom I always seem to be in conflict?
   - Do particular types of situations upset me?
   - Are there certain approaches that put me on edge?

5. How do I handle being wrong?
   - When was the last time I apologized to someone?
   - When I realize I am wrong, do I apologize right away or do I procrastinate?

6. Do I hear repeated comments concerning my behavior? Examples:
   - "I told you not to say anything!"
   - "I knew you were going to cancel."
   - "You are always late."
   - "I knew this would make you angry."
   - "If you are so upset about it, why don't you do something about it?"
   - "I wish you'd quit talking about . . . and actually do something about it!"
   - "I heard your opinion the first time. Please don't bring it up again."
   - "This is really none of your concern."

7. Do various people regularly seem surprised that I am upset with them? Do I hear comments such as:
   - "Don't be so sensitive."
   - "Are you still upset?"
   - "Come on! When are you going to get over that?"
   - "Can't you think about anything else?"
   - "I am so tired of hearing you talk about that."

## Practice Perspective

Let's continue to review your ability to uncover unrealistic expectations and counterproductive behavior by listing three mistakes, problems, or conflicts you have had in the last year. Then ask yourself the following questions.

- Who was involved in the situation?
- What was the problem or issue?
- What was my initial reaction?
- How did the other people involved react initially?
- Was there any denial in how I initially viewed the problem? If so, what was it?
- What was the outcome of the situation?
- What approach(es) did I take that seemed to help the situation?

*After* finishing this book, answer this question: What strategies would I use today to solve the problem?

> **Being honest with yourself leads to positive change! Change may be uncomfortable, but it is always worth the effort.**

# Choose Confidants Wisely

---

*Confidant: a friend or associate in whom
one confides personal information*

---

People like to talk, particularly about their problems and
possible solutions. Voicing concerns and brainstorming
options can be valuable problem-solving tools. Unfortunately,
many people misunderstand, *and misuse*, these tools. They end
up discussing their dilemma with anyone who will listen, or they
discuss their problems with inappropriate people or at the
wrong place or time.

*Bill was viewed as a real "up and comer" at his company. A new
position was being developed, and many thought he was a cinch
to fill it. During the development period, a competitor was also
courting Bill.*

*Bill's career stock started to fall when he began indiscriminately
seeking advice among his coworkers. He wasn't sure if the new
position was really going to come to fruition; what had they heard?
He was worried that someone else might be seriously considered
for the position; had they heard any other names being mentioned?
He was anxious about passing up the opportunity with the competitor; what did they know about that firm?*

*His loose talk made its way back to his boss, along with the infor-
mation that he was considering leaving the company for another
opportunity. This raised concerns with management on several
levels: Was this young man really dedicated to the company, or
was he just searching for the highest bidder? Did he have the skills*

*to be discreet in discussions about sensitive subjects? Finally, his indiscriminate advice-seeking made him appear indecisive.*

*The new position was ultimately put on hold for several months, and the other company never made him an offer. With his reputation a bit tarnished Bill decided to make a lateral move to another company about six months later.*

Bill's career questions were sound, but his decision-making process was not. He would have been much better served to seek advice from one person who understood his background and the decisions he was facing. There were several people in his company, and within the industry, who were excellent role models: smart, discreet individuals who were always happy to see others succeed. One of these people would have been a perfect brainstorming partner.

Whispering into *too many* sympathetic ears has several potential pitfalls:

- It is a safe bet that almost everyone will have a different opinion. These conflicting opinions will do nothing but confuse you.
- The more people who are privy to your business, the higher the odds of your life story being filtered to others you would prefer not to be 'in the know'.
- The time you spend explaining your situation to multiple listeners takes away from the time you have to actually work toward a solution.
- Too much talk and too little action could lead to a reputation for being indecisive and indiscreet.

Whom you choose to talk to while researching your options can be as important as the final decision itself.

## Different Situations = Different Confidants

When seeking a confidant, keep in mind that it is not possible to expect all things from one person. Take a good look at the people in your life. Strive to understand and embrace the different talents and outlooks these people bring to your table.

Be realistic. You must realize it is virtually impossible for one person to appreciate every single goal or idea toward which you strive, no matter how much he or she cares for you. *It is extremely rare to find one person in your life that is the perfect confidant for every situation.* For example, imagine your father becomes practically comatose every time you mention an acting career. He may not be the best person to look to for support or suggestions on how to reach that goal. On the other hand, your Uncle Ted, a gregarious guy who has acted in community theater, might be the perfect person to brainstorm options.

> **Gathering too many opinions will only contribute to your confusion.**

By the same token, it probably wouldn't be worth your while to drag Uncle Ted—a born technophobe—to the computer store to help you buy your new computer. But your dad. Now he's a man who, on top of being practical, is a computer whiz. He would be a perfect assistant for this practical type of quest. (You don't need to emphasize that the reason you want a computer is to keep in touch with your theatrical agent.)

*Twenty years ago a friend, Cloe, was on the lookout for a new business opportunity. While in the "new opportunity" mode, Cloe always researched anything and everything that piqued her interest. She became fascinated by a franchise that sold all-natural cosmetics. The downtown area of Denver was just beginning to be restored, and she was confident that a store of this type could be a huge success. Her interest was high enough that she contacted the franchise for information and researched retail rents in the soon-to-be- renovated downtown area.*

*Her brand-new husband, who had been out of town for a week, called home the evening she received the franchise's information* *packet. At this point, she had been considering her new idea for only two days. Yet, immediately after saying "hello" she blurted out, "Do you know there is a cosmetic store franchise that is only $300,000? And you can still get rental space downtown for reasonable rates."*

*Her husband took this news to mean she had already written a check. His response was a very simple but incredulous, "What?" Cloe was indignant that he would be so negative. Her husband was upset because he thought she was sending them to the poorhouse. The conversation went downhill from there.*

Cloe is a creative thinker, her husband is more logical. When she shared her thoughts, he assumed she was definitely going to pursue her idea. From his perspective, this was a natural assumption because his thought process is to think things through before he shares his ideas. When he discusses an idea, it is well thought out. Cloe is just the opposite. Although she has an excellent track record of making solid decisions in the end, she needs to think out-loud as part of her decision-making process.

Does this mean Cloe shouldn't talk to her husband about her goals? No, it just means she can't expect him to be the person who will sit and listen to every idea that pops into her head. Her unbridled enthusiasm makes him nervous, and it is not fair for Cloe to place him in this uncomfortable situation.

Once she understood these differences, Cloe sought out two friends who are happy to sit and listen to her myriad of ideas. These two confidants clearly understand the difference between brainstorming and actually implementing an idea. When the Great Idea has taken form, however, Cloe's husband is the first person she goes to for assistance with the practical implementation of her idea.

## Different Views = Different Advice

Discussing problems and possible options can be a powerful decision-making tool. However, you must listen to advice with the understanding that people's opinions are formed through *their* experiences, *their* interests, and *their* concerns, which may be dramatically different from yours. When choosing a confidant, keep in mind:

- People's opinions are shaped by their personal experiences. There will be many people who simply don't have an ability (through no fault of their own) to understand your ideas or concerns.
- A mature person recognizes and accepts good advice even though it may go against his or her personal desires. Don't dismiss someone as a confidant simply because you don't agree with his or her advice. Your goal is to get honest, realistic feedback. Listen with an open mind to both the positive and the negative advice you receive.
- It is not uncommon for someone who does not understand your ideas, dreams, or goals to think that your idea is a bad one. You could then find yourself wasting precious energy wondering why the person is so negative. Getting angry is counterproductive. Consider the feedback to decide whether any of the concerns are valid. If not, move on.

> **It is unfair of you to expect one person to be able to share your enthusiasm for every dream.**

## Suggestions for Being a Confidant

- If someone comes to you for advice, but you feel uncomfortable about being a confidant in that situation, say so. Excuse yourself from the role by explaining the reason for your discomfort. For example, "Tony, I can't be much help to you in this area. You should ask someone [who knows you better/understands the situation better/is more knowledgeable on the subject] than myself. I hope it works out for you."

- When you are asked for advice, and decide you are comfortable sharing your thoughts, preface your comments with the reminder that your

  **When it comes to friends or coworkers save yourself some trouble by only offering advice when you are asked.**

  outlook may differ from your friend's because of your differing life experiences.
- Try to place yourself in the shoes of the person seeking your counsel. Be supportive yet honest. Consider the following:

*Your sister has been flitting from one job to another ever since graduating from college. You, on the other hand, have succeeded in your field. You are extremely pragmatic, whereas your sister is creative with a capital C. She comes to you one day with yet another idea for a business. Your initial reaction is, "Here we go again." After her proclamation about this great new business venture, your conversation may go something like this:*

**YOU:** *How are you going to support yourself while you are building the business? This seems to me to be one more idea that you will walk away from in three months. Why don't you just get a job for a while and make some money?*

**SISTER:** *You are always so negative about everything.*

Now, think about how you can be your pragmatic self while at the same time encouraging the creativity you admire in your sister. A sample conversation:

**YOU:** *Interesting idea. Do you have a timeline for when you might open this business?*

**SISTER:** *No, I just thought of the idea. What do you mean by a timeline?*

Responding to her enthusiasm with one calm, innocuous question allows your sister to maintain her enthusiasm. It shows that you are excited for her, but your pragmatic side is still visible in asking for her timeline.

Perhaps you are too close to your sister—and too familiar with her usual pattern of abandoning projects—to offer realistic advice. How would you say so while still being supportive?

> **YOU:** *You are tremendously creative, but I simply do not have an ability to understand your ideas very well. You know how logical I am. It is probably better if you share your thoughts with someone who understands these types of ideas more clearly. But you know I am here to help you when you are ready to get started on the actual hands-on part of the business.*

As social creatures, we will always need confidants. As you become more confident in seeking your own counsel, however, your desire for multiple opinions may well disappear.

# Develop Empathy
## *(But Show It Selectively)*

---

*Empathy: the ability to identify with another's emotions*

---

Empathy is an important component in handling difficult situations. Empathy can help you predict how your decisions will affect others and help you recognize when it's best to stay out of situations that are none of your concern.

## Caution! Your Decisions Can Impact Others

No person is an island; our behavior and choices usually impact others in some way. It is up to you to make sure that the decisions you make don't cause undo stress for a coworker or friend.

*A client of mine had worked for the same company for over four years. The company had announced the possibility of layoffs, so he knew it was time to begin sending out resumes.*

*Callie & Sons, a company he interviewed with, requested a list of all past employers, including his current employer. He provided this list without much thought. Within a week, a coworker in personnel informed him that a letter requesting his employment records had arrived from Callie & Sons. The problem was that the only person who could approve that request was his immediate supervisor—the same person who was in charge of deciding who would be laid off. This request came through on a Friday, and my client's coworker said he would wait until Monday to process it.*

*The client was in a panic when he contacted me about the situation:*

**CLIENT:** *I know that my current supervisor won't be happy. In fact, it could be that I'll be chosen to be laid off because I'm looking for a new job.*

**ME:** *What do you want to do about it?*

**CLIENT:** *I'd like to call Callie & Sons and ask that they rescind the request for my records.*

**ME:** *When do you think you could actually contact someone at Callie & Sons?*

**CLIENT:** *Not until Monday.*

**ME:** *How long do you think it would take them to respond?*

**CLIENT:** *Probably a while.*

**ME:** *Well, what is going to happen to your friend in personnel if Callie & Sons doesn't rescind the request? The letter is dated. Won't your supervisor wonder why your friend held on to it for so long?*

**CLIENT:** *Oh, you're right. Well, I can't put my friend at risk. I guess I have no choice but to let the letter go through.*

Think carefully about how your actions will impact others—before taking action.

> **Be aware that your decisions could negatively impact others.**

## Neutrality Is Underused

I'll admit it. I have watched every *Brady Bunch* episode. If you want to learn how to remain neutral in a conflict between two other people, a good role model is Alice, the housekeeper. At regular intervals Mr. or Mrs. Brady would turn to her and say, "Don't you think I'm right, Alice?" Alice would dutifully pretend she was dusting and say, "Gee, Mr. [Mrs.] Brady, I really don't know."

One of the hardest lessons to learn, but one of the most valuable, is to never agree with an opinion voiced in anger by a friend concerning a disagreement with a boyfriend, girlfriend, best friend, roommate, parent, sister, brother, etc. People usually make up. When they do, somehow memories often get turned around to where *you* were the one who said all the horrible things about the husband, sister, roommate, or whoever:

> *John's roommate, Steve, had an argument with his girlfriend. For two hours Steve ranted about how his girlfriend often took advantage of him. John listened and sympathized, saying things like, "Yeah, I know. Yeah, you're right." He was only trying to ease his friend's angst, not express his opinion of the girlfriend. Big mistake. He should have said right then and there, "I'm sorry you are having trouble. But I don't really want to get into the middle of your fight. Maybe you should just call her and talk about it." But, he didn't. Within two days Steve and his girlfriend were back together, and John was viewed as the bad guy because Steve misinterpreted his sympathy as meddling.*

We feel good when people trust us enough to confide their problems to us. Don't let feeling needed allow you to become involved in a situation that is none of your business.

> **People usually make up—without any help from you!**

## Empathy Can Also be Shown through Silence

At times a negative or unkind remark directed at you has absolutely nothing to do with you. The only way to handle these types of 'slights' is to choose silence.

> *When I was in high school my best friend, Polly, and I both tried out for the Precisionettes Drill Team. The winners' names were posted on the gym door. Neither of our names was on the list. I was disappointed, but the rejection hurt less because Polly and I were in the same boat.*
>
> *Later that day Polly was summoned to the counselor's office. One of the girls on the team had to drop out, and Polly was next in line. She was a Precisionette and I wasn't! I was devastated.*

*Rehearsals for the next school year began in midsummer, when I was to spend two weeks at Polly's house while my parents traveled. I felt sick to my stomach on the first day of practice. I was jealous and feeling guilty about being jealous. My behavior toward Polly, as the unfortunate lightning rod for my disappointment, was less than honorable.*

*At sixteen, Polly had the remarkable maturity to realize I wasn't mad at her. She understood that to ask what was wrong probably would only make things worse. So she handled the situation with diplomacy and kindness.*

*At 2:00 on that fateful afternoon she got up from the couch and said, "See ya." She quietly removed those coveted pom-poms from the front closet and left. Upon her return, she immediately stowed the pom-poms in the closet. She then said something like, "Let's go to the mall." Not once during the entire two weeks did she ever talk about practice or gossip about the other girls. She was such a good friend, she didn't want to add to my disappointment. (As for me, I was a bratty sixteen-year-old who was not mature enough to tell her it was okay to talk about how exciting it was to be on the team. But that's another story.)*

Polly had every right to confront me about my nasty behavior, but she understood that I was not angry with her, I was angry at the situation.

When in doubt about how to respond to another's troubles staying quiet is usually a safe approach.

# Determine Desired Outcome

---

***Desired:*** *right for the purpose; sought*

---

B efore deciding *how* to approach a problem you must first decide *what outcome* you really want. Words once spoken are very difficult to take back. Initial reactions are often unproductive and can exacerbate a problem. Therefore, do not respond until you are confident that your actions will lead to the result you desire. Let's review a couple of common scenarios where a person's initial reaction could be unproductive and lead him or her down the wrong road.

> **Decide what outcome you are seeking *before* you take any action.**

## Dislike Your Job

**Emotional reaction:** I can't take this one more week. I quit!

**Practical response:** Okay, I don't like my job. How am I going to change my situation? No income, even for a short period, would be financially devastating. I must find a new job before I quit this one. Plus, I know it is usually easier to find a new job when you have a job. I'll start watching for new opportunities but will not to do anything formal until I have at least two months' salary in a savings account. Being proactive, even in a limited way, will do a lot to make me feel in control of my destiny.

## Dislike a Coworker

**Emotional reaction:** The next time he speaks to me, I am going to scream, "Shut up! You drive me crazy!"

**Practical response:** Losing my temper would be professional suicide. This person annoys me primarily because he talks all the time. I don't work directly with him, but see him two or three times a day. He doesn't do anything really inappropriate, he just rubs me the wrong way. I don't have to like all my co-workers, but I do have to be polite and professional. So, my best course of action is to be more tolerant of his idiosyncrasies. To get out of having a long talk with him, I'll be honest but cordial: "I'm sorry I don't have time to talk. I have work to do." I'll be polite, but I do not need to apologize for not wanting to chat.

## Encumbered by a Negative Person

**Emotional reaction:** I'll screen all my calls to avoid talking to Bridget. If I do bump into her, I'll make up excuses why I can't make plans with her. She'll get the idea after awhile.

**Practical response:** Bridget feels that I am her friend. I won't feel good about myself if I simply ignore her. It's time to take an honest look at our relationship. Do the positive things she brings to the relationship offset her negativity, or is all I get out of the relationship is a knot in the pit of my stomach? Depending on what I decide, I could:

- Leave the situation alone and let the negativity roll off my back.
- Have a heart-to-heart talk. Perhaps pointing out her negativity will help change her attitude. I might say something like, "Bridget, your negative attitude is really affecting me. I feel a little depressed every time we talk because it seems you are so unhappy. It is important for me, and my health, to try to remain positive each day. So, I need to let you know that when you are negative it affects me."

- I could move Bridget out of my life: "Bridget, I need to be honest with you. When you are negative, it affects me. I think we need to take a break from spending time together."

Notice the value of the Time Principles in these scenarios. Spend the quiet time you make for yourself thinking about what outcome you desire. You cannot determine *how* to get what you want until you are clear *what* it is that you want.

# Choose Honesty

---

**Honesty:** *characterized by fairness and sincerity*

---

B ecause confrontation can be uncomfortable, some people choose the easy way out and avoid talking directly to the person with whom they have a conflict. Instead, they go to a supervisor, friend, or other party to report the situation.

If you are angry, hurt, or suspicious of someone, that person has a right to know. Not giving the person an opportunity to explain or to resolve a problem before you go to a third party is neither fair nor honest. You can eliminate a host of hurt feelings and misunderstandings by speaking directly with the person.

*As a flight attendant, Cecile frequently worked in first class. Before locking the first-class liquor cabinet at the end of a flight, it was her responsibility to measure and record the amount of liquor remaining in each bottle. Because serving space was limited and the airline stocked full-size liquor bottles in first class, Cecile had a habit of pouring three or four shots of each liquor into a foam cup, which she covered with plastic wrap. Doing this freed up more space to work.*

*On one flight, many of her passengers were drinking vodka or gin (both colorless liquors). At the end of the trip, Cecile poured the remaining liquor back into the appropriate bottles.*

*The next day Cecile was called into her supervisor's office. She was certain she was going to be congratulated for not calling in sick for a year. To her surprise, her supervisor said, "Cecile, I have a report that you are adding water to the liquor bottles in order not to have to measure the bottles after each service."*

*"What?" Cecile started laughing. The accusation was so ridiculous she didn't even know how to respond. She explained her behavior, and her supervisor ripped up the report. She told Cecile she had been certain the report couldn't possibly have been true, but she had an obligation to check it out.*

*The supervisor would not say who had filed the report, but several weeks later, a friend told Cecile who the person was. Cecile decided not to confront this woman because she didn't want to cause problems for her supervisor. But she steered clear of her. By her inability to voice her concerns to Cecile in a mature and honest manner, this flight attendant could have done serious, and unwarranted, damage to Cecile's career.*

## To Tell the Truth?

Everyone makes mistakes; however mature individuals take responsibility for past mistakes. You can overcome a mistake in your past a great deal more easily than you can a lie, as is illustrated by the following scenario:

**If you have something to say, say it directly to the person it concerns!**

*A young man called me on a Thursday afternoon in a panic. He had upcoming interviews with two airlines, one on Monday and one on Tuesday. His panic was derived from the fact that when he had filled out his initial applications, his fear of not being competitive had led him to leave off two traffic violations he had incurred over the past four years.*

*I explained that the traffic violations were now the least of his troubles. If the potential employer discovered that he had not been totally truthful, his ethics are now suspect. If he had lied about that situation, they would reason, what else might he be hiding?*

*He agreed and decided to write out an explanation to present at the interview. He decided to apologize for the exclusion and just take whatever came his way. We spent an hour or so discussing how he should word his apology. When we were finished, he was obviously relieved to have reached a decision to tell the whole truth—or so I thought.*

*The following Wednesday, he called me back. "Well," he said, "I really blew it." Over the weekend he had listened to some bad advice. He had decided for the Monday interview that he would not disclose the driving violations. Unfortunately for him, the Monday interview was with the airline for which he had wanted to work for his whole life. By Monday night he realized he had messed up, so he told the truth during his second interview on Tuesday. This interview was with his second-choice airline.*

*Both carriers extended job offers. Now, however, he was afraid to accept the offer from his first-choice airline because he was fearful the traffic violations would be discovered during his background check. I agreed that this was a realistic fear, and his only option was to call the first airline and admit he had not informed them of the tickets. He decided it was worth a shot.*

*He called me back later and said, "Well, I was right. I blew it." He had called the head of the hiring department of the first airline and told him the whole story. The man had listened without comment and then said he would call my client back shortly. Within an hour he phoned to say, "I'm sorry, but we are rescinding the job offer. We cannot accept your approach of not informing us completely when we asked these specific questions."*

Yes, we all make mistakes, but don't compound your mistakes by adding dishonesty to the mix.

_____

# Implement Decisions Promptly

---

*Implement: to carry out*

---

Time Principles 1 and 2 (three-minute time-out; wait twenty-four hours) are designed to hold you back. Time Principle 3 is designed to push you forward. When faced with a problem or issue, *procrastination is your worst enemy.*

- If you're angry or hurt and you hold it in, you are only going to become angrier or more hurt.
- If you must confess to a mistake, waiting will do nothing but make the mistake appear worse.
- If you must have a difficult conversation with someone, waiting will do nothing but ruin your sleep and give you a stomachache.

**Time Principle 3: Implement a 72-hour deadline.** You will normally know what you need, or want, to do within seventy-two hours of thinking through a problem. Once you have decided on a course of action, implement your decision promptly.

*When I first began dating my future husband, he had just bought a 1966 Jaguar. This car was his pride and joy. He had it painted with the original Jaguar paint. He never drove it; it sat in the garage covered with a thick car cover.*

*One day I had to pick up something at his house while he was out of town. It was snowing heavily, so I pulled my car into the garage. In my haste, I opened my door too far and whacked the Jaguar's door. Looking under the car cover, I discovered that I had knocked off a huge chip of the new paint.*

*I was beside myself! I didn't really know him well enough then to know how he might react. How was I going to pay for the damage? Luckily for me—or so I thought—the car wouldn't come out of hibernation for several months. I had time to plan.*

*For the next several weeks, I fixated on my mistake. I couldn't enjoy my job, going to the movies—anything! (Yes, I was overreacting). I began having heart palpitations every time he opened the garage door. Finally, I'd had enough. One evening during dinner I looked at him and said, "I'm really sorry but I scratched the passenger door of your Jaguar."*

*He looked up from his dinner and calmly shrugged, "Oh, that's okay. If you look on the other side, I did the same thing."*

*All that agony for nothing.*

**Dealing with a problem is usually less agonizing than worrying about it.**

Use whatever means you must to rally yourself to implement your decision. If it helps to tell a confidant of your final decision in order to make yourself adhere to the 72-hour principle, then tell.

*A friend told me about a consultant her school district had hired prior to her arrival. It was obvious to her that this consultant was not doing his job, and that she would have to fire him. "I told my supervisor that I was going to do this," she told me, "not because I needed her permission, but because I knew if I didn't tell someone I would never do it."*

You can't avoid conflict. You can't avoid problems. You can't avoid making mistakes now and then. What you *can* avoid is extended periods of agonizing.

Time Principle 3 helps you guard against procrastination. Yes, do your homework, gather your facts, think through your options, write out the pros and cons but, remember, you are trying to solve a problem, not write a research paper.

# Listen to Intelligent Instinct

---

*Intelligent instinct: a natural response to a stimulus based on training or past experiences*

---

Your gut feeling, what I call *intelligent instinct,* is an important tool when searching for a solution. Of course, you want to weigh your gut instinct against the facts and a realistic view of the problem. If, however, your gut instinct is still waving a red flag once all the facts are in, take the time to notice it.

> *Twenty years ago I won a raffle. The prize was unbelievable: seven nights for two in a London luxury hotel! As my husband is not a big fan of London in the winter, we agreed that I would invite a friend to accompany me.*
>
> *Even though the hotel was paid for, there was still the matter of airfare. The one friend who had the time off and the money for airfare made me a little edgy. Although we were good friends, we are different in several very basic ways. I am a morning person; she is a night owl. She takes forever to get ready; I have designed my look (such as it is) to be able to jump from bed to breakfast table in ten minutes. I need time alone; she is incredibly, continuously social. I was nervous about how we would travel together, but I figured, "We're adults. We can handle it."*
>
> *Fast forward to five days into our adventure. It is late afternoon in the heart of London. Two American women are sitting behind a bus driver on a double-decker bus. The dark haired woman is*

*sitting stock still, arms folded, mouth clamped into a straight line, listening intently to her companion. Her blonde seatmate sits about an inch away, wagging her finger while talking in hushed, angry tones.*

*Just moments before, the woman with dark hair (me) had finally had enough. "You know what?" I had just remarked, "If you are having such a crummy time, why don't you go home early. In fact, I'll buy the ticket!" My companion was in the process of telling me that she was having a crummy time because I was so bossy. (Me?)*

*About that time the bus driver turned to us and said, "'scuse me laydees. Mighten I suggest you both could use a touch of brandy?" Fellow passengers nodded their agreement.*

*Oh, my. The emotion drained out of the moment. We stumbled off the bus at the next stop and had two brandies each. We were on our best behavior for the rest of the trip, but we have never traveled together again.*

Gut instinct is a natural and useful response: a fact I recently relearned.

*While on safari in Botswana we were camped on the edge of the Kalahari Desert. We slept on raised beds in small canvas tents. The 'bathroom' was about 20-yards from the tent.*

*I awoke late one night in need of this 'bathroom'. I stepped outside my tent into absolute darkness—my flashlight beam not offering a great deal of comfort. About ten yards away from the safety of my tent, all the hair on my neck and arms stood straight up and my heart rate increased by 50 beats per minute.*
*I stood stock-still to listen, but heard nothing. The bathroom was no longer important and I scurried back to my bed.*

*The next morning there were lion tracks surrounding our camp.*

Whether in the natural jungle, or the civilized jungle your gut (intelligent) instinct usually has something important to tell you!

# Plan Your Delivery

---

*Plan: a method or program for carrying out an objective*

---

There is truth to the saying "if looks could kill, I'd be dead." More than 90% of communication is nonverbal. *How* you say something is at least as important as *what* you say. It's easy to rationalize, "Oh, I can't say what I really think—people always take it the wrong way." False. Very often the reason people take comments the wrong way has to do with *how the message is delivered.*

Picture in your mind someone you don't like. Perhaps there is just something about this person that rubs you the wrong way. Now picture him or her standing in front of you, arms folded, face snarling, with an attitude of pure confrontation, saying, "_____ (Your name), I *cannot* figure out why there is so much tension between us. I was wondering do *you* have any ideas?"

Now imagine the same person having called you up the previous evening and asking if you have ten minutes to chat the next day. You set a time. He or she is now sitting in a chair in front of you. Calmly and with a complete focus on you, the person says, "_____ (Your name), I cannot figure out why there is so much tension between us. I was wondering, do *you* have any ideas?"

Even just writing these two scenarios, I feel calmer with the second. The words are exactly the same, but the outcome is likely to be completely different because of the person's delivery.

When you discover the resolution to a problem, don't short-change yourself by implementing it in an ineffective manner. Let me share some tips for having a productive discussion.

## Practice

Early in my consulting career, I found myself faced with a situation where I had to confront an employee about inappropriate behavior. Being nervous, I spent a lot of time thinking about what I was going to say. I thought and thought—and thought. After a while my words started sounding pretty good—in my head.

When I sat down to counsel the employee, I became flustered. The wonderful words I had played over in my head were *not* coming out the way I wanted them to. It was then that I realized that even if my words sound good in my head, they would sound different when I verbalized them for the first time.

> **Knowing what you want to say before you start talking is *never* a negative!**

After this fiasco, I began to write out exactly what I want to say. I always practice a difficult conversation in front of a mirror. It is amazing how much this little trick has helped me. I am able to recognize where my words are too harsh, my tone of voice accusatory or my facial expression condescending. I am also able to anticipate where the other party might raise a question or disagree with me; this allows me to think in advance about how I should answer. Once I began employing this trick, I found difficult conversations with coworkers and employees didn't leave me panic-stricken.

## Set a Comfortable Tone

The words you choose to introduce a subject can really set the tone for the entire conversation. Visualize how you would react to each of these openings:

▶ *"Bob, we have to talk about a problem* **you** *have."*

▶ *"Bob, I have a concern I'd like to discuss."*

The first comment immediately places Bob on the defensive by placing the blame on him. In contrast, the second comment introduces the topic in a more neutral manner instead of immediately accusing Bob of "having a problem."

## Limit Your Opening to Two Minutes or Less

Locate a clock or watch with a second hand. Now, sit still and time two minutes. It's a long time isn't it? More than enough time to get your thoughts across. If you take more than two minutes to introduce a particular problem or issue, you are likely repeating yourself. Making the same points repeatedly will only frustrate your listener.

> When discussing a conflict, never deviate from the issue at hand. Bringing up past conflicts and mistakes is no fair.

## Make an Appointment

If you give advance warning that you need to talk, the other party is less likely to feel "ambushed." Most people have an inkling when something is wrong anyway, giving notice of the conversation is a courtesy.

## Stick to the Issue at Hand

When airing your concerns stay focused on the current issue. If the conversation wanders into rehashing old conflicts, tensions will escalate.

## Follow the Chain of Command

At times you will discover that you cannot resolve a problem directly with the person with whom you are in conflict. In this case, the next step toward resolution may be moving up the chain of command. In a professional setting, going through the chain of command may mean asking a supervisor to mediate. If you decide to take this step, let the other person know your intentions. Blindsiding is never productive.

> ▶ *"Bob, I don't feel we are getting anywhere. What I suggest is that we go and speak to our supervisor together."*

If your issue is purely a personal one, choose a mediator that both you and the other person respect.

## Write a Letter

Some situations are so emotionally charged that they are impossible to talk over. Or, perhaps you've tried talking face-to-face but the conversation went nowhere. This is a time to rediscover the lost art of letter writing. You can vent all your emotions in writing the first draft. Then, a day later reread what you wrote and rewrite the letter.

You'll most likely find the second draft to be calmer, less caustic, and less littered with adjectives and exclamation points. By the time you have completed the third draft you probably will have hit on the exact emotions you are trying to describe. This draft (usually the final one) should be more reasonable and focused on the problem at hand. Consider this scenario:

> *Ann had a birthday dinner with her family. Tom, her new boyfriend, was supposed to meet her parents for the first time. Tom never shows up at the party and never calls. A day later he leaves a message on Ann's voice mail claiming he didn't come to the pary because he was too nervous about meeting her parents.*

### First Draft (Written the Night of the Party)

tom (small letters for small people)

When scientists want to clone the world's biggest idiot, they will use your DNA. Prior to bestowing you with diplomatic powers, whoever was your Maker must have had the universe's worst migraine.

You embarrassed me in front of my friends, and worst of all, in front of my parents.

There is NOTHING you can say to me that will EVER, EVER change my opinion of you. You are the Mr. Universe of LOSERS!!

Don't ever talk to me again.

—Ann

## Second Draft (A Day Later)

Tom

I have not taken your calls because I wanted to work through my initial anger towards you. Interestingly, my anger has done nothing but grow. Doubly interesting, I find you more and more repugnant as I relive that night.

You embarrassed me in front of my friends, and most distressing, in front of my parents. Your behavior was boorish to say the least.

You are an idiot.

—Ann

## Third and Final Draft (Two Days Later)

Tom:

Your behavior toward my friends, my parents, and me was, to put it mildly, horrible. You made what should have been a wonderful evening of friendship and celebration into a night of embarrassment and humiliation.

Mature, caring people never try to make excuses for immature, uncaring behavior. Your apology was weak and your reasoning frightfully immature. For these reasons I am severing my relationship with you.

—Ann

Although some of you may feel a temptation to send the first letter, believe me, with the advantage of hindsight you will feel much better about having sent the third letter.

Another bonus of taking the time to write out your thoughts is that you may discover that after a few days you are calm enough to talk to the person face to face. Either way, remember to stick to the seventy-two hour principle.

# Move On

---

***Move:** To make progress, advance*

---

My parents had a dog named Motor. Motor always had to have the last word. It seemed physically impossible for this dog to allow anything to end. She was a notorious barker, and the routine was always the same:

The doorbell would ring.

*MOTOR: Bark, bark, bark, bark, bark!*
*DAD: No! Stop barking!*
*MOTOR (looking at my father): Bark! Bark.*
*DAD: No! No barking. Bad dog!*
*MOTOR (mumbling): Woof. Woof. . . . Woof.*
*DAD: That's it!* **No barking!** *Bad dog!*

Motor would look calmly at my father and say nothing.

Three minutes would pass and Motor would say, under her doggy breath, "Woof."

Funny when it's a dog; annoying when it's a person.

When you have made your decision, discussed your decision with those involved, and the last word has been said—drop it and move on! Put "The End" at the end of the problem. Make your point once, clearly—and allow the conversation to *end.*

## Forgive and Then *Truly* Forget

When you accept an apology, understand that your chance to talk about the problem is over.

Many times we have difficulty forgiving because we never honestly told the other person how we felt. Thus, there is a constant, nagging desire to replay the situation in your mind with you saying exactly what is in your thoughts and in your heart.

The first step toward being able to forgive *completely* is to be honest right from the start. Don't say, "It's no big deal," if it is. You will be surprised at how much more quickly true forgiveness will come if you explain your feelings in a straightforward manner right from the beginning. Do yourself a favor; let people know, calmly, how you honestly feel.

> *A friend made an embarrassing comment about me in front of a large group of friends. I knew she didn't mean it and that I should just forget it, but I couldn't. Finally, I called her and said, "I just have to let you know that your comment really upset me. I hope that you will be just a bit more careful in the future." The minute I shared my true feelings, I was no longer upset.*

## Apologize

The moment you realize you have made a mistake, say "I'm sorry" and do what you can to rectify the situation. Delaying making an apology only allows hurt feelings to simmer and stew. Once you have apologized, sincerely and with feeling, drop it.

## Forgive Yourself

I have discovered that we are all capable of making ourselves feel much worse than anyone else ever could. To take a line from a classic bestseller, "Be your own best friend." If your best friend was sincerely upset over a mistake she made you would never consider telling her how stupid she was or how poorly she handled the situation. No, you'd say things like, "You made a mistake, and we've all done that." "You are being much too hard on yourself."

I wonder why we are so good at giving this type of encouragement to others, but we can't seem to offer it to ourselves. Yes, review your behavior, learn from your mistakes, but make sure you forgive yourself.

# Case Histories

The more you practice a skill, the more proficient you will become; improving your decision-making and problem-solving abilities is no different. With this in mind, I have provided scenarios of challenging conflicts or decisions for you to review. By noticing how the twelve strategies were applied in the following scenarios perhaps, when you are faced with similar circumstances in your own life, you will be better prepared to handle the situation.

## The Twelve Strategies

# Scenario 1

---

A young man realized he was having an excessive number of conflicts with his coworkers.

---

The young man came to realize that when he received negative feedback about his work, his initial response was to be sarcastic and condescending. With his new insight, he decided to apply the Time Principles whenever someone critiqued his work. He resolved not to respond until he had taken time to sift through the comments.

By removing his initial emotions he gradually learned to examine people's comments objectively. He was able to recognize when people had terrific ideas versus when their feedback missed the mark. Because he did not react instantaneously, he was able to be calm and professional, either thanking the person for the ideas or discussing his reasons for disagreeing with them. After several months, he saw his conflict count with his coworkers diminish greatly.

## Strategies Used

1. Build a Solid Foundation
2. Use Silence Effectively
3. Seek Perspective
4. Recognize Unrealistic Expectations
8. Choose Honesty

# Scenario 2

A forty-seven-year-old woman was having difficulty making friends at her new job.

After some review, she came to the realization that she was overly sensitive. This job was her first outside the home in more than ten years. She began to understand that she was so nervous about doing a good job that every little comment ("Sue, could you please note the time when you take a message?") felt like a scolding from the principal. She admitted to herself that when she was rebuked for anything she became uncommunicative.

Her first step toward diminishing her sensitivity was to watch how other people interacted. Looking outward she realized that the feedback she received was reasonable—and that she rarely made the same mistake twice. By taking an outward view, she saw that everyone in the company got their fair share of such feedback. Once she was able to look at the big picture, she was able to control her sensitivity. She even discussed this revelation with two trusted coworkers. These co-workers became more understanding of her reaction and seemed to be impressed that she was working on self-improvement.

## Strategies Used

1. Build a Solid Foundation
3. Seek Perspective
4. Recognize Unrealistic Expectations
5. Choose Confidants Wisely

# Scenario 3

A young college student was told by one of her close friends that she was completely undependable.

This young woman came to the realization that she said 'yes' to every request. As a result she would become overwhelmed and regularly back out of events and favors at the last minute. Her last-minute cancellations showed a lack of respect for other people's time and had given her the reputation of being unreliable. By taking an outward view, she learned that she needed to become comfortable saying 'no'. Her inward view fairly screamed that when she said 'yes', she had better follow through on her commitments.

## Strategies Used
1. Build a Solid Foundation
3. Seek Perspective
4. Recognize Unrealistic Expectations
7. Determine Desired Outcome

# Scenario 4

A young professional felt as though his coworkers were avoiding him.

This individual was a committed community activist with little patience for people who were not willing to become involved. Through taking an outward view, he realized that in his dedication to his beliefs, he often chose the wrong time and place to voice his opinions or to start a conversation. No wonder people were starting to avoid him! He quickly came to the conclusion that work was not the place for such conversations. He stopped trying to initiate political conversations at the office. His coworkers, over time, became more comfortable and open around him.

**Strategies Used**
1. Build a Solid Foundation
3. Seek Perspective
6. Develop Empathy
7. Determine Desired Outcome

# Scenario 5

One young woman confided that she felt her boss and co-workers did not take her seriously.

This woman constantly felt that people dismissed her ideas. She came to understand that she appeared to lack conviction. If *she* didn't believe in her ideas (as her approach seemed to indicate), why should others believe in her? She decided she must speak up with more enthusiasm. She knew she didn't think well "on her feet" because she became too nervous. Her solution was to organize her thoughts and write them down. Then during staff meetings she could share her ideas with confidence. Within several months she felt more confident in presenting her work ideas and her coworkers were listening to her with more interest.

**Strategies Used**
1. Build a Solid Foundation
7. Determine Desired Outcome
11. Plan Your Delivery

# Scenario 6

One woman was told she was not a good friend.

Ruth told Sally she was not a good friend because she never reciprocated Ruth's dinner invitations. Sally reminded Ruth that she had cared for her animals while she was traveling, but Ruth's irritation did not diminish. Ruth obviously had strict expectations about how someone should show friendship. It was clear to Sally that Ruth constantly set herself up to be displeased. Although they remained cordial, Sally chose not to spend a lot of time developing the relationship.

**Strategies Used**
1. Build a Solid Foundation
7. Determine Desired Outcome
10. Listen to Intelligent Instinct

# Scenario 7

A young man had been fired from two jobs in as many years.

A young man made an appointment with me to figure out the reasons for all the job terminations. During our first conversation, he disagreed with a point I was trying to make (concerning something I can't recall). I tried several times to explain my reasoning, but he continued to argue, challenging me with, "That doesn't make any sense" and, "How could you possibly come to that conclusion?" After several attempts, I succeeded in explaining my reasoning. Instead of saying, "Oh, yes, now I see your point." He said, "I get your point, move on." Obviously, he had no idea how to admit he was wrong. Clearly this behavior was one factor contributing to his inability to stay employed! We had a long conversation about my initial reactions to his behavior. He finally came to realize that he, in fact, had a problem with being too argumentative. He left with a desire to begin to add the twelve strategies into his daily life.

**Strategies Used**
1–12

# Scenario 8

---

Sam learned that a business competitor was using the Internet to spread misinformation about his company.

---

One day Sam found negative comments about his company on a forum for members of his profession. These comments were purportedly from one of Sam's clients, but after some research, Sam realized the post had come from a competitor. Nothing like this had ever happened to Sam before. He was furious.

His initial reaction was to respond in the same public manner, to expose the weasel and make the same type of nasty insinuations about him. He would uncover that company for the scoundrels they were! Then Sam would call the competitor and give him a piece of his mind. Yes! That's what he should do!

Instead Sam did nothing for twenty-four hours. When he calmed down, he realized that his competitor was using these tactics because his company's work was substandard. He also realized that reacting in kind would only harm his reputation. Sam decided the best course of action was to do nothing.

Within days, past clients began to respond on their own to these false statements. Within one week a retraction appeared on the site, although no one from the offending company ever apologized or took responsibility for the comments. The only reason for the retraction was to stop the tide of positive press Sam's company was receiving in response to the negative comments.

## Strategies Used
1. Build a Solid Foundation
2. Use Silence Effectively
3. Seek Perspective
10. Listen to Intelligent Instinct
12. Move On

# Scenario 9

---

Tom found his ethics challenged when a dinner guest told a crude joke.

---

At a party a guest told a crude joke during dinner. Not knowing how to respond, Tom said nothing and laughed along with everyone else. Afterward, he felt tremendously disappointed in himself and struggled to find a way in the future to express his convictions that such material was inappropriate. He wondered: What do you do when the person making the comment is entertaining you in his or her home? What do you do when the person is someone you must work with on a daily basis?

He was thankful to witness a casual acquaintance react to exactly the same situation he had faced. This individual did not laugh at the joke. Instead, he looked at the joketeller and said, "I don't understand that kind of humor. Let me tell you a truly funny story." He went on to tell a lighthearted anecdote that got everyone laughing and reduced the tension in the room. In his own quiet way, he had stated, "I will not listen to those types of comments." But, by immediately telling his own joke, he turned the attention away from the joketeller, minimizing everyone's embarrassment.

The young man began adopting this approach in similar situations, and it has never failed to stop an inappropriate conversation dead in its tracks.

## Strategies Used
1. Build a Solid Foundation
8. Choose Honesty
11. Plan Your Delivery

# Scenario 10

---

Tom hired a gregarious woman as the company receptionist. To put it mildly, she was not working out.

---

Tom decided the only alternative was to terminate this employee. He became so anxious about *how* to do so that he kept putting it off. (The problem was easy for him to ignore because the receptionist was very good at interacting with his clients; it was her interaction with coworkers that was causing problems.)

Finally, one day an employee made a complaint about the receptionist. The complaint was one Tom had heard a hundred times. He finally boiled over. He called the receptionist into his office to discuss her behavior and—well, he let his aggravation and anger get the best of him. The conversation quickly became very unpleasant and the employee left on the worst of terms.

Tom was flooded with mixed emotions. Yes, he had finally solved his problem, but he'd done it so poorly! How could he have let his emotions run away with him like that? He realized he had made the receptionist feel worse about herself than she deserved to feel.

In hindsight he realized he could have used some advice on how to handle the issue more appropriately. Tom phoned an experienced business owner whose opinion he respected. This colleague suggested that if Tom had spoken to his employee the moment there was tension, she would have (1) changed her behavior; (2) decided to find another job; or (3) given him clear grounds to terminate her. Tom could have used many of the 12 strategies to handle this situation more professionally.

## Strategies Used
1. Build a Solid Foundation
2. Use Silence Effectively
7. Determine Desired Outcome
8. Choose Honesty
9. Implement Decisions Promptly
10. Listen to Intelligent Instinct

*Case Histories*

# Practice Scenarios

For these next scenarios I do not list my suggested answers. My goal is to offer you some practice scenarios to help you plan how you may want to handle similar issues in the future. To get even more out of these practice scenarios—share them with friends. How would they handle these situations?

# Scenario 1

You have been studying hard all semester but your best friend has not. He comes to you the night before the exam and asks if you can "help him out" (i.e., cheat) during the test. If he fails this exam, he will be kicked out of school. What will you do?

# Scenario 2

You notice your boss is padding his schedule to boost his weekly pay. He is adding only two or three hours, he's a wonderful boss, and he does work very hard. What will you do?

# Scenario 3

You have an acquaintance whom you have known for several years, but you are not close. He asks you to write a letter of recommendation for him to present during his job search. You know nothing about his work history. What would you tell him?

# Scenario 4

You and your spouse play mixed doubles tennis every Saturday morning with another couple. Recently the couple has begun to bicker at each other throughout the entire match. Saturday mornings, which you and your spouse used to look forward to, have now become a chore. What should you do?

# Scenario 5

A coworker has called in sick, but you know that he is going to a baseball game. Because of his absence, you are asked to work late, but you have plans. What do you do?

# Scenario 6

The scenario is the same as number 5, but the person asked to stay late is another coworker. You are not affected at all. Is your behavior different?

# Scenario 7

A former employee worked for you for more than five years. During her employment, she had a drinking problem that negatively affected her work. You have not seen this person in three years. She recently called and left a message asking for a letter of recommendation. She is expecting a return phone call. What do you do?

# Scenario 8

You start work at a new job. One of your coworkers invites you out to lunch and immediately begins to complain about another coworker. What do you do?

# Scenario 9

You have a neighbor who constantly drops in unannounced. This interrupts your day. What do you do?

# Scenario 10

Your company is sending several employees to a convention, which requires one overnight stay. To hold down costs, the company has requested that employees share rooms. A coworker you do not particularly care for asks you to share a room. What do you do?

# Scenario 11

A friend asks you if you have heard rumors about her spouse behaving inappropriately. You have indeed heard rumors. What do you do?

# Scenario 12

You are new to the neighborhood. Your next-door neighbor's dog barks constantly. What do you do?

# Scenario 13

You just started a new job a month ago. You realize accepting this position was a huge mistake, but quitting after only a month? What do you do?

# Scenario 14

A 'friend' has told you that she heard your neighbor complaining about the noise that your children make. This neighbor has never complained to you. What would you do?

# Scenario 15

You have been told, in confidence, that your friend's department may be eliminated. What do you do?

# Final Thoughts

Though not exactly strategies, I want to mention two final traits everyone would be well served to develop: powers of observation and memory.

If you pay attention to what happens to you on a *daily basis,* you may well discover that you begin to notice problems in their infancy. Problems are much easier to resolve when they first present themselves.

Once a problem is resolved, take a moment to adhere to memory the lessons you learned. Store the solution in your memory bank. Should the same type of problem ever darken your doorway again, you will have the solution at the ready.

Remember, it is easy to be successful if nothing bad ever happens. A truly successful person is one who faces problems quickly and reviews them realistically, and then learns from the mistake.

We will all make mistakes in our lives, some pretty horrendous but the majority fairly benign. By incorporating the twelve strategies into your daily life and remembering to pay attention to the lessons adversity can teach you, you are well on your way to becoming a more empathetic person and a smarter, more effective problem solver.

As always, I am anxious to hear from my readers. If you have comments, suggestions, or criticisms, please feel free to contact me at cheryl@cageconsulting.com. Only through your feedback and suggestions can I continue to improve.

All the best,
Cheryl Cage
Tucson, Arizona

# *About the Author*

**Cheryl Cage** is the founder and president of Cage Consulting, Inc. Since 1988 Cage Consulting has provided interview preparation services to professional pilots seeking interviews with major U.S. airlines, international airlines, commuter airlines, and corporate flight departments. In addition to consulting with individual clients, Cage Consulting publishes some of the best-selling career guides in the aviation industry.

Cheryl has served as an independent consultant to the Air Line Pilots Association (ALPA), the national airline pilot union representing more than 60,000 airline pilots. In this capacity she has designed and presented interview preparation seminars to displaced pilots from PanAm, Eastern, Midway, USAirways, TWA, Aspen Airways, and West Air, to name a few. She also has conducted job-search seminars for furloughed pilots pursuing employment outside the cockpit while awaiting recall to their airline.

In 1994 Cheryl wrote her first book *Checklist for Success: A Pilot's Guide to the Successful Airline Interview.* Since then, she has written five books, published nine titles, and developed an on-line training test and interactive training CD-ROM.

*Calm in the Face of Conflict* is the second book in Cage Consulting's *Practical Strategies for Professional and Personal Growth* series. The information offered in this series is applicable to professionals in **any** field.

In addition to writing, publishing, and advising individuals facing career concerns, Cheryl finds time to be a regular speaker at colleges and conventions. Cheryl has a degree in psychology and lives in Tucson, Arizona, with her husband, Young.

# Cage Consulting, Inc.

## Products and Services

**To Review or Order Books or Receive Information
Call Toll Free: 1-888-899-CAGE (2243) or
Visit Our Website: www.cageconsulting.com**

─────────── Business Titles ───────────

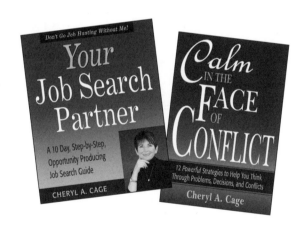

**Your Job Search Partner**
*A 10-Day, Step-by-Step, Opportunity Producing Job Search Guide*
The last job search book you will ever need.
By Cheryl Cage

**Calm in the Face of Conflict**
*Twelve Powerful Strategies to Help You Think Through Problems,
Decisions, and Conflicts*
By Cheryl Cage

# Pilot Titles

**Checklist for Success**
*A Pilot's Guide to the Successful Airline Interview*
By Cheryl A. Cage
Over 20,000 copies sold. Updated Yearly.

**Checklist CD: An Interview Simulator**
By Cheryl Cage
Applicants answer questions in a correct/incorrect manner and
Cheryl critiques. Also: paperwork, self-evaluation. 2 hours.
(Companion to *Checklist* book.)

**Airline Pilot Technical Interviews: A Study Guide**
By Ronald McElroy
Approach plates, weather, AIM, FARs, mental math, cockpit
situations to analyze.

**Mental Math for Pilots**
By Ronald McElroy
Mental math tips and tricks for interview and cockpit use.

**Reporting Clear? A Pilot's Guide to Background Checks**
By Cheryl Cage
Pre-employment background checks are an important part of the selection process. Do-it-yourself background check and reasons why you should conduct your own background check prior to filling out employment applications.

**The Resilient Pilot: A Pilot's Guide to Surviving, & Thriving, During Furlough**
By Cheryl Cage
Real-world, motivational guidance to help find enjoyable work outside the cockpit.

**Pilot E-TrainingTest: Mental Math**
By McElroy/Cage
Gauge your mental math abilities then improve them with this online mental math study tool. To order this online study guide visit www.cageconsulting.com

**Pilot Classroom Series: Flashcards**
*Vol. I: AIM*
*Vol. II: FAR 1, 61, and 91*
*Vol. III: FAR 119, 121, and 135*
By Ronald McElroy

**Welcome Aboard!**
*Your Career as a Flight Attendant*
By Becky S. Bock (Cage)
A complete guide to understanding the job of F/A and preparing for interviews.

# Notes

# Notes

# Notes